Who were the Vikings?

When Viking warriors first began their raids, they struck terror into the hearts of people. We have many descriptions of the attacks, written then or soon after, which give the Vikings a very bad name.

But the Vikings were not only fearsome warriors. In this picture you can see a rich landowner, a merchant, a craftsmen, a farmer and two ladies.

What is the merchant holding in his right hand?

What do you think he is doing with it?

Which of the two ladies do you think might be married to the rich landowner?

What do you think the craftsman does for a living?

Now colour this picture in.

You can find out more about Viking costume on pages 10 and 11.

Answers on page 16

1

Where did the Vikings come from?

G_ _ _ _ _ _ _ _ _ _

I_ _ _ _ _ _ _

N_ _ _ _ _ _

S_ _ _ _ _ _

D_ _ _ _ _ _ _ _

I_ _ _ _ _ _ _

GERMANY

Rhine

NORMANDY

Danube

Byzant

ATLANTIC OCEAN

NEWFOUNDLAND

Mediterrane

The Vikings came from a part of the world called Scandinavia.
Colour in the land between the dotted lines (. . . .) to see their
homelands more clearly.

The modern names of the three Scandinavian countries where
they came from are Norway, Sweden and Denmark. Write them in
on the map.

And where did they go?

The Vikings were great travellers. If you colour in the arrows on the map you will see the routes they took more clearly.

They attacked many countries in Europe, and later they settled in parts of Britain, Ireland and France. The part of France which they settled is called Normandy; the Normans who invaded Britain with William the Conqueror in 1066 were descended from Vikings.

They also crossed the Atlantic Ocean and settled in Iceland and Greenland. The name Greenland may have been chosen to make this new land sound attractive, but much of it was covered with ice and glaciers, and it was very difficult to make a living there.

The Vikings also discovered North America; they gave the names Helluland, Markland and Vinland to parts that we call Baffin Island, Labrador and North Newfoundland in Canada.

They also travelled east to Russia and founded colonies there. They fought in the guard of the emperors of Byzantium, and they even visited Jerusalem and Baghdad.

Write in on the map the names for Greenland, Iceland, Ireland, Russia.

In the countries they visited or settled the Vikings found goods to trade with. These are some of the goods they traded:

🛍 silver		🐑 wool	
jewellery		wheat	
walrus ivory		🐝 honey	
furs		wine	
falcons		pottery	
✕ weapons		slaves	
antlers		spices	
silk			

Look at the map and write down what they got from:

Iceland ....

England ....

France ....

Germany ....

The Byzantine Empire ....

Russia ....

Norway ....

Sweden ....

Greenland ....

Baghdad ....

Black Sea

Caspian Sea

Baghdad

Jerusalem

3

The Vikings at home

Although they did have a few towns, most Vikings lived in the
country. This is a picture of the inside of a Viking house.
They slept on the platforms on either side of the fire.

Can you complete the picture?

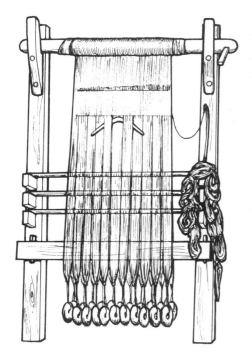

Some things which belong inside the Viking house are missing. You can see them on this page. See if you can tell what they are. Draw them in where you think they should go, then colour the picture.

1. Every household would have had one of these.

2. What would have been put in here?

3. How would the joint of meat be cooked?

4. What toys might the children have had to play with?

5. What would the woman use to stir the stew?

6. What might this jug contain?

A quiz

Look at the picture and see if you can guess what some of the strange-looking objects inside the Viking longhouse are. Answers on page 16.

1 ....

2 ....
....

3 ....
....

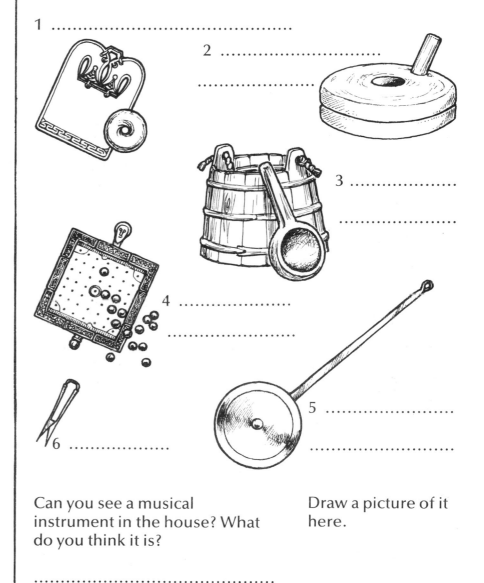

4 ....
....

5 ....
....

6 ....

Can you see a musical instrument in the house? What do you think it is?

Draw a picture of it here.

....

A Viking ship

The Vikings were renowned as sailors and were skilled at building ships. In longships like the one in the picture the Vikings travelled all over the northern world.

Finish the drawing of this ship and colour it.

Some ships had weather vanes made of bright metal, with brightly coloured streamers.

The sails were often brightly coloured in diamond patterns or stripes.

The prows of their ships were often carved as dragons' heads and brightly painted. Draw in this ship's figurehead.

Vikings gave their ships names, like Long Serpent, Bison, Strider, Crane. Name this ship and write its name in runic letters on the prow. You can find how to write in runes on page 12.

There were holes in the sides of the boat for the oars, but when they were in harbour the Viking warriors might line the sides of the ship with shields. You can draw in some shields, and paint them in bright colours.

The sailors carried their personal possessions in trunks, and they sat on these when they were rowing. Draw in the sailors' trunks.

Fresh drinking water would have been carried in barrels – don't forget to add them to the ship.

Viking ships did not have holds – the merchant ships carried their cargo and the animals in the central part, where the deck was lower.

Pagans . . .

At first the Vikings were pagans – they worshipped many gods. Some of the days of the week in English are named after Viking gods. Can you guess which ones?

Thor was a warrior god. He was also very stupid. He had a hammer which became his special sign. Here it is.

People used to wear pendants of Thor's hammer to protect them.

Write Thor's name in runes on the hammer. You can find out how on page 12.

Match up the names of the days with the names of the gods:

Tuesday	Thor
Wednesday	Frey
Thursday	Ty
Friday	Odin (or Woden)

Odin was the chief god. He carried a spear, had one eye and two ravens – Huginn and Muninn – which whispered secrets to him. What do you think he looked like? Draw a picture of Odin and his ravens in the space below.

and Christians

Later the Vikings became Christians but for a long time they still kept their old way of life.

This picture is of a cross from a churchyard at Middleton in Yorkshire. Although it is Christian it has a picture on it of a Viking warrior with all his armour. Can you recognise a helmet, a knife hanging from his belt, a shield, a sword, an axe and a spear?

Colour the picture.

The Vikings in Britain

In 793 the rich monastery of Lindisfarne in Northumberland was destroyed by pagan men who came from the sea. No-one had ever experienced anything like this, and nobody knew where the Vikings had come from.

A Northumbrian priest called Alcium wrote about the raid:

For nearly 350 years we and our ancestors have lived in this lovely land. Never before has such a terror come to Britain as this that we have suffered from a heathen race. Nor was it thought possible that such an invasion could come from the sea. Behold the church of St Cuthbert, spattered with the blood of the priests of God, robbed of its ornaments.

Find Lindisfarne on the map.

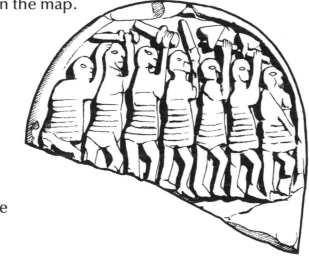

This broken stone from Lindisfarne commemorates the raid.

About 70 years after their first raids, the Vikings began to settle in Britain. The parts where they settled are coloured grey on the map. Some of the Vikings who came to Britain were Norwegian, but the most important groups were Danes. They controlled a large part of north and eastern England, called 'Danelaw'.

How do we know where the Vikings lived?

You can sometimes tell where the Vikings lived by some of the things they left behind. This stone was found in London. It dates to the time when the Danish king Canute the Great ruled most of England and Scandinavia.

It was a memorial stone from a Viking burial, but we don't know who it commemorates. It has a picture of an animal, with a snake twisted round its front legs; over its back is a decorative pattern. The animal was painted black with white spots, the border and snake were dark red and the background white. See if you can paint it in the right colours.

What else did the Vikings leave behind?

SHETLAND ISLES

Jarlshof

These are just some of the things you can go and see.

At **Jarlshof** in the Shetland Isles are the ruins of a Viking farmstead.

Viking jewellery from the **Orkneys** and **Hebrides** can be seen in the National Museum of Scotland in Edinburgh.

Some churchyards have Viking stone crosses. You can see such crosses on the **Isle of Man**, at **Gosforth** in Cumbria, and at **Middleton** in Yorkshire.

Near **Cuerdale** on the banks of the River Ribble in Lancashire a Viking treasure chest with silver ingots and over 7,000 silver coins was found. The treasure is now in the British Museum.

At **York** part of the Viking town has been dug up and many fascinating things have been found. Find out more about York on pages 14-15.

In **Saffron Walden** Museum in Essex is a decorated silver pendant which was found in a cemetery nearby.

In **London** Viking weapons were found in the mud beside London Bridge and are now in the Museum of London.

How else can we tell where they lived?

You can sometimes tell by the names of places. This drawing is of the area around Alford in Lincolnshire: find it on the map. We know that Vikings lived here. The names underlined are Scandinavian. How can we tell? Answer on page 16.

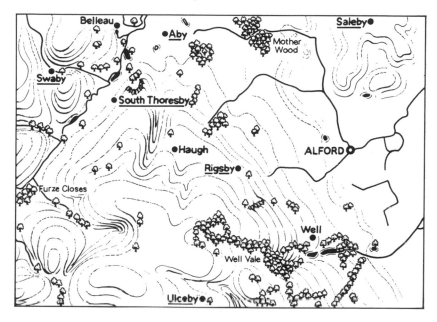

The Vikings in Ireland

The Vikings only settled parts of Ireland, but from the end of the 10th century Dublin was the most important Viking trading town in the west. There are rich Viking finds in the National Museum in Dublin.

Viking dress and jewellery

The Vikings were proud of their appearance, and liked to show off their wealth with fine clothing and jewellery. The material was usually made of wool or linen. It was woven at home by the women and dyed in attractive colours. More expensive materials, like silk from the east, could be bought from merchants. Both men and women wore jewellery.

Men wore trousers which were held up by a sash or a drawstring. On top was a straight tunic, worn with a belt. In winter heavy cloaks would be worn over the tunic. Shoes or ankle boots were made of leather.

Finish the picture of the man by copying the drawings on this page. The jewellery has been drawn larger to make it easier to copy. Colour the picture.

All free men had the right to carry weapons, and even at home a Viking would usually have a dagger, a spear or a sword. When they went into battle Viking warriors were well armed, and they fought bravely. Their main weapons were the sword, spear and axe. They defended themselves with large circular shields, which were made of wood, and were often painted in bright colours. If they were rich they might wear steel helmets and mail-chain to protect themselves.

spear

helmets

He needs a **brooch** to fasten his cloak.

Finger-rings were popular.

Axes were common. Sometimes the axe-head was decorated with complicated patterns.

Some men wore **neck-rings** of gold or silver.

He might wear a **pendant** with magic powers for protection.

The Vikings' swords were deadly weapons, with very sharp edges. They were slung from a baldric carried over the right shoulder and held in a scabbard.

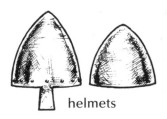

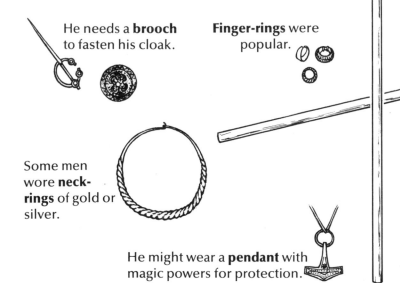

10

Viking women wore long linen dresses. These could be either plain or pleated. Over the dress was a long woollen tunic, a little like an apron. It was held up by a pair of brooches. These were sometimes joined by a chain or string of beads. Over the tunic they could wear a shawl or cloak, fastened with a brooch or a pin.

On this page you can see some of this lady's jewellery – it has been drawn larger to help you copy it. Finish the picture and colour it in.

Necklaces with beads and pendants were popular.

A pair of **brooches** to fasten the tunic.

Other brooches could be worn on the dress or shawl.

Women as well as men wore **finger-rings**.

Arm-rings and **bracelets** were also worn.

Women carried the household **keys** on chains hung from a belt or from a brooch.

Dress up as a Viking

Make a cloak from a large square of coloured material. Fasten it at the shoulder or across the chest with a brooch.

Make a lady's tunic from two rectangles of material joined at the top with ribbons. It should reach half-way between your knees and ankles. Wear it over a long dress, and fasten it at the top with two large brooches.

You can make a Viking brooch. Cut an oval or a circle from stiff card. Colour it gold or silver, and draw on a pattern if you like. Fix a safety-pin to fasten it on the back using sellotape or sticky plaster.

The Viking alphabet

The Vikings had their own alphabet called the futhark (or futhork). The letters in the futhark are called runes. The Anglo-Saxons used runes too, but they were not quite the same as those of the Vikings.

There were several different versions of the futhark. Teach yourself runes with this one. Practise copying them in the spaces below. Then send a runic message to a friend.

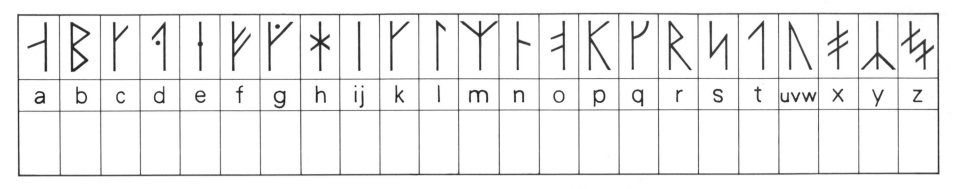

a	b	c	d	e	f	g	h	ij	k	l	m	n	o	p	q	r	s	t	uvw	x	y	z

Runes were cut with a knife or sharp point on to wood, stone, metal or bone. Sometimes the Vikings practised the alphabet on pieces of bone or wood, like the animal bone in the drawing below. The first 6 letters give the alphabet its name. Can you recognise the others? Write them in the space below – the difficult ones have already been written in.

Sometimes the runes gave an owner's name. The letters on the back of this brooch spell: **Malbrithaastilk**. This is written in the Old Norse language and it means: 'Melbrigda owns (this) brooch'.

Below is a picture of a fine carved bone comb. But who does it belong to? Write the owner's name in runes in the space at the top.

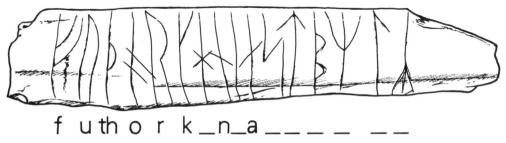

f u th o r k _ n _ a _ _ _ _ _ _ _ _

Some runes just give the name of the man who wrote them. They often used the words: _ **risti runar**. This means: '_ cut these runes'. Try writing in runes _ **risti runar** using your name instead of the dash.

The picture below is of a memorial stone. The design on it shows a twisted animal.

Can you see its head? There is a plume coming from the head which is twisted round the body. It looks like this:

It is tied up with a ribbon that looks like this:

Its tail looks like this:

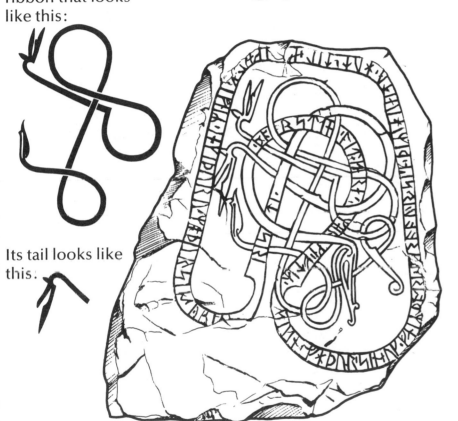

Inside the body of the animal are runes. They are written in Old Norse, and they say:

Torsten caused this monument to be made in memory of Sven his father and of Tove his brother who went out of Greece and of Ingatora his mother. Ybber engraved it.

This is a picture of a snake from another memorial stone. Can you see the plume coming from the snake's head? It is twisted round the tail.

There should be an inscription inside the snake's body, but it is missing. What do you think it might say? It could tell about the wealth of a chief or the good deeds of a woman.

Make up an inscription and write the runes in the snake's body. There is probably enough space for about 60 letters. Try it out on a piece of paper first.

Jorvik – the Viking city of York

In 866 Vikings captured the rich Anglo-Saxon town of Eoforvic. The Vikings called it Jorvik, and for 200 years it was the capital of a Viking kingdom. Under the Vikings it became richer, one of the most famous cities in Britain. Its merchants brought luxury goods from far away – from Europe, Scandinavia and even from the East.

In an area of modern York called Coppergate archaeologists have discovered part of the Viking town. They dug up what was left of some of the Viking houses. And they found many things that the people who had lived there had left behind – jewellery, combs, pieces of material (they even found a woollen sock!), coins, and all sorts of household goods, such as cups and bowls, buckets, keys and so on. From these the archaeologists can get an idea of what life must have been like in Viking times.

A Viking street scene to cut and colour

This picture shows you what the front of some of the Viking houses may have looked like. Colour it in and cut round the outline. Cut a strip of card, 25 cm by 4 cm. To make the houses stand up, fold back the flaps and stick them to the card. On the next page are some figures to add to your scene.

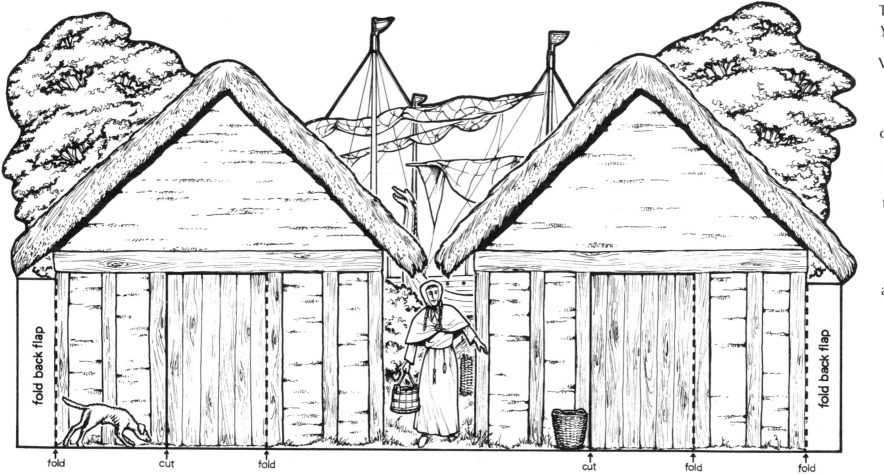

The houses were packed closely together, and the streets were narrow. There were small alleys between the houses, running down to the river. There were no paving stones, and the drains were open. Rubbish was thrown into the yard or trodden into the street surface. Viking York must have been a very smelly place!

The figures on this page show some of the kinds of people you may have met in Coppergate in the 10th century. Look for:

a blacksmith
a wood-carver
a jeweller selling his goods
a man carrying fish

To complete your scene, colour the figures and cut them out. Stick them on to a strip of card, folded over at the base, so that they stand up.

At the Jorvik Viking Centre in York you can travel back in time and visit a model of the Viking town as archaeologists think it may have been.

The people who lived in the houses at Coppergate were craftsmen and their families. They sold their goods on stalls in front of their houses.

From the things they found, the archaeologists could work out what crafts were carried out here.

There were bone and antler-carvers. They made things like combs and knife-handles.

Wood-workers made cups and bowls.

Metalworkers made jewellery and weapons.

There were leather-workers and glass-makers.

In one of the houses coins were minted.

Who's who?

The Vikings did not have surnames like we do, but were called after their fathers. So a man called Erik Haraldson had a father called Harald. His daughter Astrid would be called Astrid Eriksdaughter.

Here is a picture of Sweyn, Olaf and Erik with their sons.

Follow the threads to match up each father and son. Then finish the boys' names.

Sometimes Vikings had nicknames. The nicknames of Sweyn, Olaf and Erik are Bloody Sword, Thick Legs and Seal Head. Can you tell which is which? Write their nicknames in above them.

Here are some more Viking nicknames. Draw a portrait of:
Ketil Broken Nose
Kirstin Red Eyes
Olaf Hairy Breeches
Ingrid Starry Eyes.

What other nicknames can you think of?

Sweyn   Olaf   Erik

Sigurd   Jon   Ketil

.... son   .... son   .... son

Answers

Who were the Vikings? (page 1)

1. The merchant is holding a pair of scales for weighing money.
2. The lady on the left is married to the rich landowner – she has a lot of fine jewellery.
3. The craftsman is a blacksmith – he has a hammer, tongs, and an anvil.

Inside a Viking house (page 5)

The objects are:
1. A loom: Viking women spun wool and wove their own cloth at home.
2. Valuables were locked in the wooden trunk for safe-keeping.
3. On a spit over the fire.
4. The children's toys are: a wooden sword; a model boat; a toy duck.
5. A wooden ladle.
6. Wine; the jug is imported.

Quiz

1. We are not completely sure, but we think that the board and the glass weight may have been for smoothing or ironing cloth.
2. A quern: it was made of two round stones and was used for grinding grain to make flour.
3. A wooden bucket and a ladle.
4. A game board and counters.
5. A griddle iron for baking bread over the fire.
6. A pair of shears.

The musical instrument is a flute.

The Vikings in Britain (page 9)

We can tell which are the Scandinavian names, because they end in the letters -by.

Other Activity Books from the British Museum

The Ancient Egyptians
The Ancient Greeks
The Anglo-Saxons
The Arabs
Britain before the Romans
The Eskimos
The Romans

Drawings by William Webb

© 1987 The Trustees of the British Museum

Published by British Museum Publications
46 Bloomsbury Street, London WC1B 3QQ.

Reprinted 1987, 1988

Typeset by Rowland Phototypesetting
(London) Ltd,
30 Oval Road, NW1 7DE
and printed in Great Britain by
St Edmundsbury Press Ltd,
Bury St Edmunds, Suffolk.